ELEGY FOR A LOST SON

poems by

Joanne Linn

Finishing Line Press
Georgetown, Kentucky

ELEGY FOR A LOST SON

Copyright © 2018 by Joanne Linn
ISBN 978-1-63534-687-9 First Edition
All rights reserved under International and Pan-American Copyright Conventions. No part of this book may be reproduced in any manner whatsoever without written permission from the publisher, except in the case of brief quotations embodied in critical articles and reviews.

ACKNOWLEDGMENTS

Publisher: Leah Maines
Editor: Christen Kincaid
Cover Art: Joanne Linn
Author Photo: Robert Linn
Cover Design: Elizabeth Maines McCleavy

Printed in the USA on acid-free paper.
Order online: www.finishinglinepress.com
         also available on amazon.com

                Author inquiries and mail orders:
                      Finishing Line Press
                          P. O. Box 1626
                  Georgetown, Kentucky 40324
                            U. S. A.

Table of Contents

A Voice Was Heard in Ramah 1

Poem for Ben 1

For Ben 2

Thursday 3

Blue 5

Seeds 6

Mother's Lament 7

Loss of a Filling 8

Mammahugs 9

Too Early 10

Birthday Poem for Ben 12

Fading yellow Roses 13

Here's to You 14

Love Poem for my Lost Son 16

This Body I Wear. 18

Old Woman 20

Potlucks and Playgroups 21

October Tag sale 23

for Bob
for Bobby and Jared
and for
Benjamin Walter Linn
June 9, 1987 – December 8, 2016

A VOICE WAS HEARD IN RAMAH,
LAMENTATION, WEEPING, AND
GREAT MOURNING,
RACHEL WEEPING FOR HER
CHILDREN,
REFUSING TO BE COMFORTED,
BECAUSE THEY ARE NO MORE.

        MATTHEW 2:18

Poem for Ben

I wish that I could follow you
as the gulls soared through the air,
their white feathers glinting against
the hot sun of a summer day—
follow the trail of their winged flight
as they followed
the wake of a fishing boat
in Gloucester, after a catch.
They sought nourishment,
Yet attained flight.
How short the season of your blooming.
How eternal the sea
and my memories.

Perhaps our son's soul soars
In spheres not yet seen.

For Ben

The yellow-gold of the new forsythia blossoms
herald the newness of this, our first spring without you.
My tears, the sadness in your father's eyes,
cannot do justice to the loss of you.

How to go on,

knowing that you would want us to thrive and flourish—
live lives as lush and full as the lavender blossoms
of the hydrangea that was given to us
after creating the white and purple quilt square
that bears your name.

How to go on, we ask,

when the daffodils and tulips beckon to us of early spring.
They call to us and remind us
of the all-too-short season of your blooming.

How to go on,

living in this coffin of loss?
I long to embrace you and instead
can only fold these lonely arms around the burnished urn
that holds the remains of your dear body.

"I am not here," I hear you calling.
Not there, yet you turn in memory to face me,
smiling, with newly shorn hair.

Thursday
for Ben

I woke this morning to a sky
as gray as slate,
even though it is early spring.
My fingers reach for the sugar bowl,
seeking
                                    any
sweetness for my coffee.
The bowl is made of Depression glass—
gold
shading to orange
and then to red,
colors warm as the sun on the day
of the late summer book sale—
when you, with arms made strong by
heavy lifting,
scooped up the unsold tomes
to carry to the car.
Where to find sweetness
now,
on this, the fourth month
of your death?
Yesterday the couple upstairs passed us,
wearing radiant smiles, and waved.
His arm was wrapped around
her shoulders.
Where are your father's arms,
that used to hold me so close?
During these four months
I have been forced to learn
a new language, learned
to converse in another,
                                  not mother—
tongue
as I inhabit a world without
you.

Where are you now,
who once took root in my womb?
I seek,
yet cannot find you.
Turn to look and see
only the sky, cold, gray—
and face yet another day.

Blue
for Ben

Blue—both color and state of being.
When pale it speaks to us of sky—
full, at times, of feathered flight.
There is also a darker shade of azul ,
a hue reminiscent of some oceanic depth,
and also the color of the earrings that
were one of your last gifts to me.
These I treasure beyond measure.
Scent is one of the last of the five senses to go,
a woman once told me.
I remember, and reach inside my closet
for the cloth, a pillowcase.
Cloth, yet more than cloth.
I bury my face in it, also blue,
still permeated with the scent of you.
I recall the day in late August
a few short months ago,
leaves shimmering in a hot summer wind.
the dog still with us.
"I will find you a nice girl to straighten you out,"
my friend Rose joked, smiling.
Now you are gone, all three.
Naught remains, save leaves.
Not a trace of you remains—
not on the bench upon which you sat,
nor in the grass you once trod.

Seeds
> *for Ben*

I wake this morning to find that it is Earth Day,
a mere span of time.
Twenty-four hours set aside,
set aside to celebrate the turning of this, our earth—
set aside to honor the omnipresent changing of the seasons.
It is now spring, the season in which even soil changes its color.
First dark brown, then to newly sprouted green.
Spring—also the changing of bud to blossom.
We gather, your father and I,
with a small group of people for planting,
and share our seeds—
seeds of herbs and purple forget-me-nots.

Forget-me-nots.

No danger there is of forgetting.
I wake each morning lush not with visions of leaves and petals,
but rather with a heart full to bursting with the grief and pain
of losing you.

What to do?

We sow seeds.
I write poems.
We consider adopting some furred friend, a feline.
Would this, perhaps, bring some solace to our pain?
Help, somehow, to fill the emptiness occasioned
by the loss of you?

What to do?

Write poems.
Plant seeds,
with sorrow forever furrowed,
deep within the depths of my soul.

Mother's Lament

My soul desolate,
heart pierced each day anew
by the anguish and pain of losing
you.
Soul, heart—both laid waste,
bereft,
laid bare by the knowledge
that never again
will you walk this world with me.
Never again,
my son.
You who once I carried
warm and safe
within my womb.
Would that I could
have kept you there,
yet birthed you,
too soon,
on the ninth day of June.
In what unfathomable, unseen realm—
not ephemeral, no doubt eternal,
do you now dwell?

Loss of a Filling
for Ben

I wake
to face
my grief.
Eating breakfast
a filling falls,
drops from some damaged tooth.
Upon examination
it has split,
the dentist declared,
split
as the trunk of a tree might be
if struck by lightning.
I ponder both—
tooth and heart—
each one broken,
torn apart.
The remnants of my tooth
are removed.
I know that one
will heal.
One, but only one,
gum,
not heart,
splint, torn, rent in two—
forever broken
by the grief and pain
of losing you.

Mammahugs

Welcome home, our furred friend,
not solution but solace
to this,
our new-found solitude.
We grieve for our son.
I chop onions on the cutting board
that he gave to me,
bamboo.
You
settled right in, my husband said.
Surely you must once have belonged
to some other family,
inhabited a different home.
Surely they must have loved you,
but did not spay you.
How many babies did you bear,
our new brown tabby?
Which pain worse—that in your womb,
giving birth—
or the one in your ear,
drum popped,
cancer eating away at a lobed edge?
Cured now, divest of kittens,
we offer you our love
and give you kindness and care.

Too Early
     for Bob and Ben

Too early,
rudely,
we are awakened.
The phone rings,
brings news of Trumpcare,
a healthbill passed
by ruthless Republican politicians.
Too early
for talk of politics, I think,
and blink,
eyes half-opened.

Too soon yet to start
another day, gray,
filled with rain
and thoughts of your death.

Your father's test is Monday.
Will there be enough breath
left in lung?

I have already lost you—
son and dog both.
Not him, too.
Who would then there be
to love and comfort me?

Later on we lie down to nap,
all three—
husband, cat and me.
Tired, yet I lie awake
and wait
to hear the words that will not come,
"I'm all right now, Mom."

Unable to rest,
yet I hesitate to rise.
I do not want to disturb her,
for precious is her presence.

She gives me pause,
this new cat of ours,
as she tentatively approaches,
coming ever closer,
with her small, striped body
and delicate paws.

Birthday Poem for Ben

"Happy Birthday, Baby."

Friday was your birthday.
You would have been thirty
had you lived.
Your father shared with me
a memory
of some summer long ago—
a vacation
taken
with your older brother
and grandmother.
We were bound for Nantucket
carried there
by the sea.
En route to our rented cottage,
outside,
you spied
the wild brown rabbits.
Perhaps only two,
you
set about contstructing a trap.
You
gathered wild wisps of leaves,
added grasses, lettuce and branches
from some small tree.
A lair—
made with such care,
crafted by my little boy,
so precious and so funny,
who only wanted a bunny.
Six months now since your death,
daily I know fear and
as Conrad once wrote,
"a grief too deep for tears."

Fading Yellow Roses
    —*Mothers' Day, 2017*

Fading yellow roses,
and my first Mothers' Day
without you.
A gift from one of your brothers,
their freshness now is slightly spent—
and yet their color still lights up
our apartment.
Their scent is diffused in these
two rooms.
Fading golden roses
on a day so cold and gray.
Lunch and yellow roses—
on this,
a different Mothers' Day.
I cannot help but love them,
for they are my sons—
the ones
who gave these gifts to me.
Once there were three,
now only two—
and where are you?
Pain now sears both feet and heart,
one ideopathic neuropathy,
the other everlasting grief.

Here's to You
> *for Ben*

"Here's to you, my rambling boy—
may all your ramblings bring you joy." —Tom Paxton

Once you rambled
in wild woods.
You navigated the forests,
and parted the branches,
through the thickets and
brambles
of childhood.
We often went camping,
traveled to one bluegrass festival
or another
put up a tent,
staked our claim—
you, me, your father
and two brothers.

Years later,
again you rambled—
but not through forest thicket
or bramble.
Rather there was the
   beat
      beat
         beat
of your feet
on concrete,
on city streets,
headed, perhaps, to a bar
and some "chick" you hoped
to meet.

Yesterday your father and I
went to a ballgame
in July heat.
Old now, less able, stricken with grief—
we could not find the car,
could not find you.

Did we walk the same Hartford streets
that once bore the prints
of your dear feet?

My mind now rambles,
roams and travels,
down through the days
when it was
you
who played
football,
lineman for the Chargers,
our little dog a mascot
for the team.
I recall your smile,
your strong legs,
your love,
and thoughtful ways.
Now you have died
and I cry.

Matter cannot be created
or destroyed.
So, here's to you,
my rambling boy.
May your spirit,
unencumbered by your body,
bring you joy.
May it ramble
where it will—
ramble through wild wood
or city street,
over the earth
and through the sky.
Know that I
will never say
"Goodbye."

Love Poem for my Lost Son
for Ben

Last night your father and I went out to see a beautiful sunset.
The sky had turned pink, behind the buildings, above the trees.
I was not there the day you died.
I could not see the same light that was in the skies
leave your eyes.
Were you alone
In your new home?
It was a house, but not a home, not yet—
you once wrote of this, of house and home
in your poem.
I was out, delivering Christmas cards.
How could I have known?
Did you suffer,
my dear and wayward son?
Was there anyone
in that room, by your side?
Would that I could have been the one who was—
to hold you and console you,
to hold your body in my arms,
a body as dear to me after your death
as it was on the day that you were born.
I tried so hard to keep you safe from harm.

I saw my father's face and looked at his closed eyes
as he drew one final breath.
Saddened then, but not bereft.
For him it was time.
He was old, had suffered pain.
How could I know that,
later, I would be left,
inconsolable—set so adrift by your death.

I carry you with me now, everywhere,
still not quite knowing how to feel you near.
You were the one to my heart so dear.
I wear a vial with some of the ashes
from the burnished urn
that holds the remains of your dear body—
around my neck and close to my heart,
always and forever—no longer apart.

This Body
for Ben

This body I wear
used to bear
babies,
three of these.
Grown now,
two are young men
I rarely see.
You are gone.

    You of the generous spirit.
    You who were patient.
    You who were kind.

I seek the holy mountain
from the depths of the valley of doom.
You left too soon.

Does your spirit still walk
through the grasses,
stalk
around these buildings,
rustle through leaves,
hear the cries of the loon?

This body I wear
now bears
the immortal wound.
A wound unbandaged,
a wound untended,
a wound that gapes,
a wound that turns gangrenous
with each word heard,
uttered by a white man
in a white house.

It is a wound that burns
with each new death, and
by knowing that you were left
alone
to draw one last breath.

This body I wear
does not reside
by the mouth of the River Congo.
It has no Nkonde,
guardian of collective memory.
It has no nails of malediction
and cannot utter any benediction.
Like the immortal wound
the war machine grows ever larger.

This body I wear
has eyes that see
and they bleed.

Once one sees,
one cannot unsee.

Old Woman
Post-election, November 21, 2016

I see tombstones all around me.
Cancer eats away at ancient bones.
Colostomy bags, conjunctivitis, oxygen tanks.
Fetuses unborn and yet to be born.
Fathers, mothers, take care of your children.
A friend, old woman, quakes in fear—
quivers like an aspen tree in this cold November wind.
Her own mother survived the Holocaust,
carried away in a straw-lined carriage to the camps.
Yet the sky, the stars and our dogs still sing to us.
They sing, they cry, they wail, they scream—
"Rise, rise, try again!"
Mothers and fathers, sons and daughters,
lost or gone.
Yet other days, other trees, who are our grandmothers,
still stand straight and strong.
They say, "Go on, go on."
'Till we can no more.

Playgroups and Potlucks

Two gatherings of women,
groups,
each
a gaggle of geese,
gossiping.
Who is out?
Who is in?

My mind travels
back through years
and unshed tears,
for we were not
the chosen ones—
not me, not my small son.
Yet we were the ones
talked about
by those three women,
young—
with their poverty of spirit
and lying tongues.
The lies they told
marked friendship's end.

The years unravel.
Time has elapsed.
Much has happened.
A new gathering of women,
another group.
Five old women
who agree to monthly meet,
ostensibly to share
small-talk and supper.
Who is out?
Who is in?
Where to begin?

We are not the chosen ones,
again,
not me, not my man.
I do not understand,
but know within
that we are talked about
with words that wound
like a whetted knife.
"Get a life," I want to say.
For the talk of women
should not hurt,
but rather mend.
I face another
friendship's end.

October Tag Sale
for Ben

Your father and I went to East Granby
and drove through streets
        with leaves
        turned red and gold
        a filigree
leaves that looked soft
        as feathered flowers.
At a yard sale we stopped
and I spied
a bicycle.
No longer able to ride,
Other things I sought.
We stopped and I bought
a framed poem
that reminded me of you.
I read it with tear-glazed eyes,
chose a rug,
some small jars for herbs,
went home and forgot—
these chosen things replaced
by other people,
other thoughts.

Late at night I woke,
after dreaming of the bicycle
I had bought for you—
aware anew
that you have died
and it is you that cannot ride.

Does your soul still glide,
soar by trees, fly the skies?

Elegy for a Lost Son, written by **Joanne Linn**, is a compilation of poems written after the loss of her deeply loved son, Benjamin. These poems are her way of paying tribute to him and are also an exploration of the first year of her grief process. They are written from her heart and it is her hope that they may touch your hearts also.